FREDDIE
THE FARTING SNOWMAN

JANE BEXLEY

ISBN 9798554499067

Did you know that everyone has gas? Kids toot. Dogs toot. Even snowmen toot!
This is Freddie and he farts A LOT. In fact, Freddie passes so much gas that there are names for all the ways he toots.

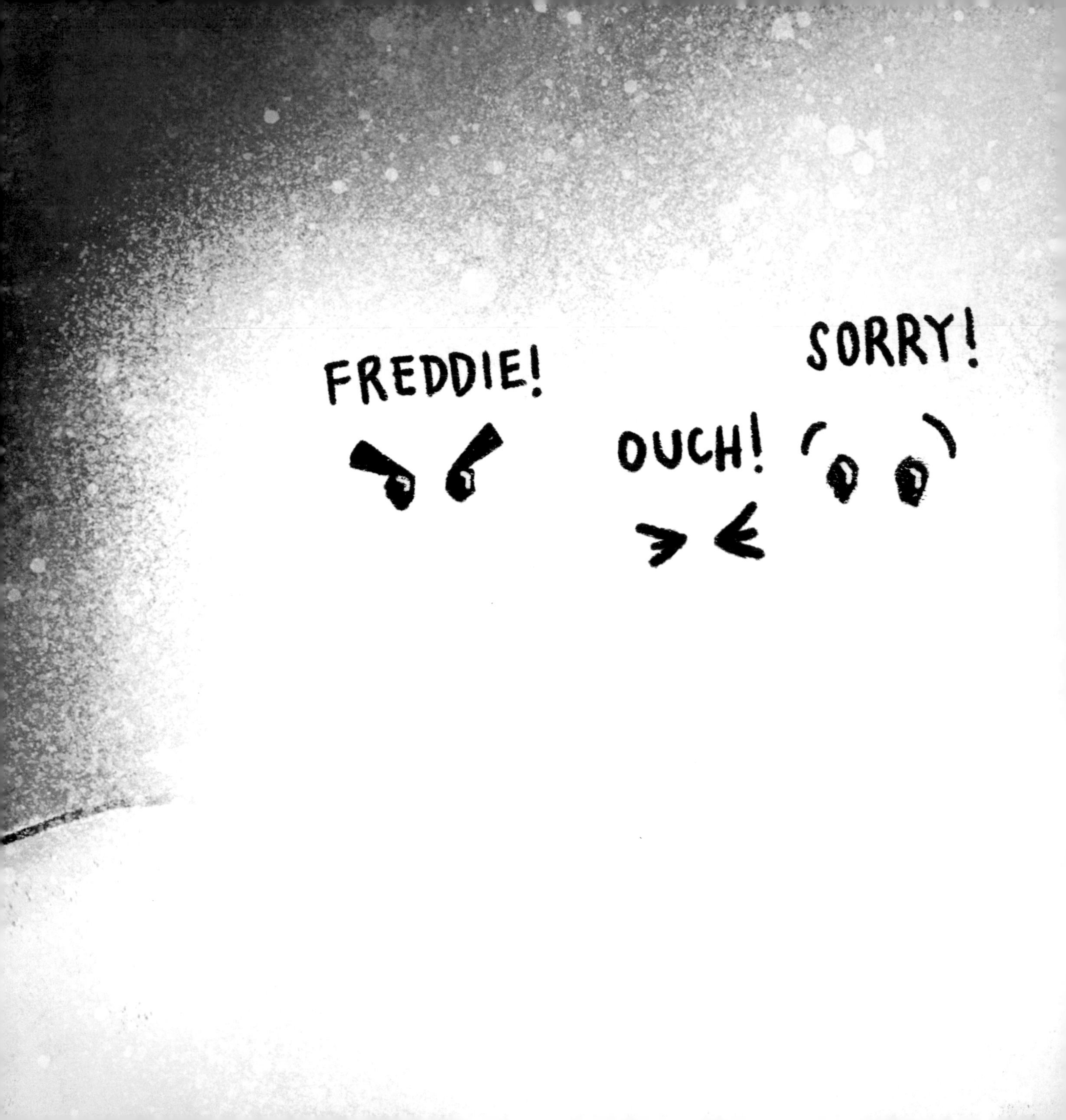
FREDDIE!
OUCH!
SORRY!

TOOTING THE GLUTE FLUTE

Tooting can be a fun musical activity. Freddie loves Tootin' the Glute Flute with his buddies.

THE FARTSICLE

On the coldest of cold days you might get lucky and see Fartsicles! These frozen fluffs are Freddie's favorite farts.

THE ARCTIC BLAST

This powerful fart will send you flying across the snow-covered hills if you aren't holding on to something.

THE RUMP ROOSTER

A Rump Rooster is a loud fart in the middle of the night with enough cracking power to wake you up.

TOOT-A-DOODLE-DO!

JURASSIC FART

Cover your ears and run! Jurassic Farts are huge gas bombs with dino-sized roars and smells.

THE WIND TUNNEL

A Wind Tunnel is when you toot somewhere with people stuck behind you. Common wind tunnel zones are escalators and moving walkways.

THE POOT

Sometimes you need to fart in fancy places. You should try to use tiny toots called Poots to be as quiet as possible.

THE SMELLFIE

If you ever want to smell your own toots, just do what Freddie does and take a Smellfie. This is when you wave your fart towards your face and take a big, deep sniff.

BUM SHAKERS

These vibrating and odorless toots are felt, not smelt.

THE SNART

A Snart is when you sneeze and fart at the same time. Snarts are pretty rare which makes it really exciting to catch one!

Passing gas by yourself can be pretty fun. But Freddie knows that tooting is best when you share the fun with your friends.

Made in the USA
Coppell, TX
05 September 2023

21220132R00021